Dori James is one of t[illegible] always been in the b[illegible] takes place at Spoken Word. Being a woman of few words, the words that she does speak hold weight in the spirit. I believe that this book was published as a result of Dori's faithfulness over the little things in her life. God has intervened and caused her to rule over much. When I was told that this book was accepted by a publisher I was elated. But when I found out that it was accepted by Charisma Media...I was proud. This book is a manifestation of generational posterity. I have been privileged to be this young woman's pastor for five years. God is so awesome that He allowed her to be promoted from my armor bearer to an author with the same company that publishes my books!

Dori has given her gift to the ministry for many projects. Her service to me, my family, and the church has been without reproach. The spiritual growth that she has received while serving in this capacity is to be modeled. I believe that her obedience to the faith has opened the doors of the Christian publishing market to her.

As you read the prayers of this book, you will experience the word of the Lord that says that the effectual (heartfelt), fervent prayer of the righteous avail much! These prayers are letters to God from Dori's heart. They are innocent, powerful, and most of all anointed! When you study and pray these prayers, you will experience three generations of power. Enjoy!

—Apostle Kimberly Daniels
Pastor, Spoken Word Ministries
Best-selling author, *Clean House Strong House*
City Council member, Jacksonville, Florida

PETITIONS
to MY FATHER

PETITIONS
to MY FATHER

RHODORA JAMES

CREATION
HOUSE

PETITIONS TO MY FATHER by Rhodora James
Published by Creation House
A Charisma Media Company
600 Rinehart Road
Lake Mary, Florida 32746
www.charismamedia.com

Unless otherwise noted, all Scripture quotations are from the Amplified Bible. Old Testament copyright © 1965, 1987 by the Zondervan Corporation. The Amplified New Testament copyright © 1954, 1958, 1987 by the Lockman Foundation. Used by permission.

Scripture quotations marked KJV are from the King James Version of the Bible.

Scripture quotations marked NIV are from the Holy Bible, New International Version of the Bible. Copyright © 1973, 1978, 1984, International Bible Society. Used by permission.

Scripture quotations marked The Message are from *The Message: The Bible in Contemporary English*, copyright © 1993, 1994, 1995, 1996, 2000, 2001, 2002. Used by permission of NavPress Publishing Group.

Design Director: Bill Johnson
Cover design by Nathan Morgan

Library of Congress Cataloging-in-Publication Data: 2012943429
International Standard Book Number: 978-1-62136-091-9
E-book International Standard Book Number: 978-1-62136-092-6

While the author has made every effort to provide accurate telephone numbers and Internet addresses at the time of publication, neither the publisher nor the author assumes any responsibility for errors or for changes that occur after publication.

First edition
12 13 14 15 16 — 9 8 7 6 5 4 3 2 1
Printed in Canada

CONTENTS

INTRODUCTION

THE PURPOSE OF this book is to reach out to the brokenhearted; to those who are downtrodden, bruised, crushed, and broken down by calamity. This book is for those who feel left out, left behind, and forgotten.

It is important that you know God has not forsaken you. He is the Deliverer with the power to make you free. He is the One that heals, comforts, and restores. It is in Him that you will find peace.

A plea for mercy:

> Have mercy on me, O God, according to your unfailing love; according to your great compassion blot out my transgressions. Wash away all my iniquity and cleanse me from my sin. For I know my transgressions, and my sin is always before me. Against you, you only, have I sinned and done what is evil in your sight, so that you are proved right when you speak and justified when you judge. Surely I was sinful at birth, sinful from the time my mother conceived me. Surely you desire truth in the inner parts; you teach me wisdom in the inmost place.
>
> Cleanse me with hyssop, and I will be clean; wash me, and I will be whiter than snow. Let me hear joy and gladness; let the bones you have crushed rejoice. Hide your face from my sins and blot out all my iniquity. Create in me a pure heart, O God, and renew a steadfast spirit within me. Do not cast me from your presence or take your Holy Spirit from me. Restore to me the joy of your salvation and grant me a willing spirit to sustain me.
>
> Then I will teach transgressors your ways, and sinners will turn back to you. Save me from bloodguilt, O God, the God who saves me, and my tongue will sing of your righteousness. O Lord, open my lips, and my mouth will declare your praise. You do not delight in sacrifice, or I would bring it;

you do not take pleasure in burnt offerings. The sacrifices of God are a broken spirit; a broken and contrite heart, O God, you will not despise.

—PSALM 51:1–17, NIV

PART I
BEING MADE IN ADVERSITY

Chapter 1

PRAYER AGAINST UNCERTAINTY

Now every athlete who goes into training conducts
himself temperately and restricts himself in all things.
They do it to win a wreath that will soon wither, but
we [do it to receive a crown of eternal blessedness]
that cannot wither. Therefore I do not run uncertainly
(without definite aim). I do not box like one beating
the air and striking without an adversary. But [like a
boxer] I buffet my body [handle it roughly, discipline
it by hardships] and subdue it, for fear that after pro-
claiming to others the Gospel and things pertaining to
it, I myself should become unfit [not stand the test, be
unapproved and rejected as a counterfeit].
—1 CORINTHIANS 9:25–27, AMP

I PLEAD THE BLOOD over my mind, in the name of Jesus. I come up
against doubt, distrust, and all lack of certainty in my life. No longer
will I embrace incertitude, being capricious, easily changeable, and
fickle. I cancel every assignment against me created to cause a waver
in my thinking. All skepticism and suspicion is renounced along with
worry and ill motives for acceptance. Let desolation and death of making
wrong decisions in my life come to an end, as well as that which comes
to impede progress. Indecisiveness, deceptive exploits, fallacious acts, and
destructive heresies, depart from me, right now, in the mighty name of
Jesus.

Protect me, O God, from a weakened mind-set. Deliver me from confusion and demonic confederacies. Cause that which is dubious to be far
from me in the name of Jesus. O God, bring balance to those things that

have been left undecided and/or unsettled in my mind. Clear me, Lord, of cloudy thinking and confusion.

Instead, make me to be sure, certain, and undeniably steadfast. Equip me with Your wisdom. Teach me Your ways. Sustain me in what is true and what is constant, that which is You. Stand me upon my feet, Lord and Savior. Establish me. Operate through me, Your will to be done. Separate me from darkness. Fortify me, O God, in You.

I thank You right now for causing the attacks against my mind to immediately subside. The bands of wickedness have been broken. No more fear, nor hesitation when You call on me to do Your will for my life. All distractions are being removed as I learn to trust You.

I ask that this trust (in You) be elevated. Cause it, O God, to expand and intensify. Teach me how to separate from my old ways. I want to trust You on another level, as You expose me to new realms, new dimensions, and different developments. In the name of Jesus, teach me how to take custody of Your trust and put it in a place where it could never be stolen, tampered with, or tainted. I trust and believe in You, Father. To You I have been made accountable for much.

Refresh me and restore me, Father. Deliver me from the opposition of uncertainty that comes to claim my mind. You are my Deliverer, my Savior, my Comforter, and my Friend. You are my Father, the One that really knows me and loves me to no end. You are my Teacher and Trainer; my Joy...my Peace. I will praise You forever. In Jesus's name, I pray.

Chapter 2

PRAYER AGAINST LONELINESS

*For He has not despised or abhorred the affliction of
the afflicted; neither has He hidden His face from him,
but when he cried to Him, He heard.*
—Psalm 22:24, AMP

I N THE PRECIOUS name of Jesus, I cancel the assignment of sadness from circulating in my life. Let every experience and every encounter be of Your good, giving birth to a positive perspective, and an onset of obedience led by a mind that finds joy in giving You praise.

In the name of Jesus, I command all legal rights of loneliness to take flight and flee far from me, at once. I plead the blood over my heart, my mind, and my spirit. I plead the blood over the words that I speak, my actions, and my deeds. I continuously renounce the spirit of loneliness as I become established in You—Your joy and happiness. I decree and declare that I have been released of all emotional suffering and pain.

I repent for reflecting upon images that have opened the door to dejection, depression, desolation, and all forms of despondency. Father, grant my future with Your wisdom. For You are my Shield and Protector. You are my soul's Provider. You are the One who delivers me.

Every spirit of sadness, loneliness, and self-pity, I separate myself from you. Instead, I will take refuge in His Word, which sustains me. Let satisfaction in the Lord be my portion and His joy forever be a part of me, in Jesus's name.

Bless me, Father, with a newfound spirit of friendliness; a communicable and unshakeable happiness that is far too good not to be shared. Allow the smile that You've dressed my heart with to show upon my face.

Let these gifts be contagious. I praise You, Father, and ask Your forgiveness of my sins. Teach me to recognize You in every situation. In Jesus's name, I pray. Amen.

Chapter 3

PRAYER AGAINST BROKENHEARTEDNESS

The Spirit of the Lord is upon me, because he hath
anointed me to preach the gospel to the poor; he hath
sent me to heal the brokenhearted, to preach deliverance to the captives, and recovering of sight to the
blind, to set at liberty them that are bruised.
—LUKE 4:18, KJV

I LIFT UP TO You, O God, my heart, and ask that You heal me of its
brokenness. Cancel the assignment of the enemy that causes my heart
to be depressed and despondent, filled with misery and mourning.
Interrupt my sadness, O God, with Your love, Your kindness...Your joy.
It is Your peace that I am in great need of.

Forgive me, Father, for every entry point through which I have
allowed the wicked one to enter. Let my mouth speak only of Your goodness, Your grace, and Your mercy. Teach me how to exchange my nega-
tive statements for positive truths, in the mighty name of Jesus. For it is
in Your presence that I choose to dwell.

I renounce every symptom of a broken heart, every ungodly manifestation and ordinance that has allowed its trespasses to take place in
my life. I decree and declare that I am no longer overcome by grief and
despair. Hopelessness is gone and sadness is no longer a distraction.

I thank You right now for mending my heart; for retrieving every
piece that has been shattered, stepped on, or thrown away. I thank You,
Father, for a heart that has been delivered and stands whole and sound
in You. I decree and declare through Your power and authority that my
heart is not fragmented, nor is it separated or made apart from You.

This day, I bless Your holy name. I thank You for setting me free from the spirit of heaviness. I thank You for demolishing every attribute associated with self-pity that has attached itself to me. I thank You for Your deliverance from depression, rejection, suicidal thoughts, grief, sorrow, excessive mourning, dejection, and inner hurts. Thank You, Father, for Your healing that comes from within.

I am washed clean by Your blood, living under Your favor, and made free to serve You on yet another level. It is because of Your goodness and Your grace that I am here today. Let wholeness and abundant living [in You] be my portion.

You are my King and my Comforter, the One who supplies my every need. You are my Eternal Father. With You, I have life everlasting. And for this, I give You praise.

With a smile upon my face and happiness in my heart, I thank You for the garment of praise and the oil of joy. In Jesus's name, I pray. Amen.

Chapter 4

PRAYER AGAINST THE
SPIRIT OF OFFENSE

But I tell you, love your enemies and pray for those
who persecute you, to show that you are the children
of your Father Who is in heaven; for He makes His
sun rise on the wicked and on the good, and makes the
rain fall upon the upright and the wrongdoers [alike].
For if you love those who love you, what reward can
you have? Do not even the tax collectors do that? And
if you greet only your brethren, what more than others
are you doing? Do not even the Gentiles (the heathen)
do that? You, therefore, must be perfect [growing into
complete maturity of godliness in mind and character,
having reached the proper height of virtue and integ-
rity], as your heavenly Father is perfect.
—MATTHEW 5:44–48, AMP

O, GOD, LET me not fall victim to the spirit of offense. Block
what has come forward to inflict bitterness, brokenheartedness,
and shame. Put a halt to those ungodly thoughts of revenge
and retaliation that reach for me by night. Awaken me, Father, daily with
the power, the authority, and the might of the Greater One that You have
placed on the inside of me.

Help me, Lord, to cast down evil thoughts. Remove wicked imagina-
tion, as I put on the armor of the Lord daily. The helmet of salvation, the
breastplate of righteousness, and the belt of truth build me up as I pray
in the spirit without ceasing.

Truth be told, I have been treated unfairly. These encounters were
unjust and were not right. For a time, I was persecuted for no reason and

punished severely by sanctions that failed to fit the crime. My enemies have been allowed to walk away freely as I have toiled for days with emotions of torment and pain.

Lied on, talked about, cheated; used, abused, left broken, and then discarded, sometimes completely misunderstood; alone, unfulfilled, and forgotten; yet in all of this, I refuse to be offended. Instead, I will cling to Your Word, and continue to bless Your holy name.

Please break the arrows that take aim at my character. Put a stop to the awful words that are said to cause me shame. Allow me to hold on to You as my Shield and my Buckler, as I take refuge in Your name; praising You, worshiping You, trusting You, and needing You. I will continue on. In Jesus's name, I pray. Amen

Chapter 5

PRAYER AGAINST RAGE

Wrath is cruel and anger is an overwhelming flood.
—PROVERBS 27:4, AMP

RAGE IS AN angry fury. It is a violent anger, destructive and turbulent in nature, that attaches itself to well wishes that are beheld by its wrath to be destroyed. It is the one that hates to see a smile or a happy face, especially as it relates to the revealing of God's goodness. Rage is an insanity of the mind toward His reign.

This spirit rushed forward to attack me and brutally beat me to a pulp. It wanted no judgment brought up against it because it desires its own fame. Rage intended to be spread out amongst the people around me like a wildfire unable to be dowsed. I tried stomping on it with my feet, but it didn't work because I did not believe. I tried to overcome it in so many other ways, but I did not prosper because I failed to give Him praise.

Rage entered through an experience that left me disgruntled; again, I failed to give Him praise. It came in repeatedly from my deliberate intent to step to the side and say nothing when wrong was being done. It was Rage that attacked me and forced me to struggle against life. It caused me to become oppressed, depressed, upset, disgruntled, and beside myself with emotional pain. Violence and torment, I thought, was the answer; feelings of agony and defeat, I thought, would never change. I did not know that being ignorant of His Word made me one of the enemy's easiest targets.

It is through many vessels that Rage wants to plant a seed of wickedness and revenge. It is furious and swift in its delivery, powerful in many of its ways. However, it can be stopped. By accepting the love of God, making a commitment to the body of Christ, and keeping my covenant with Him, I forced it to leave me.

Rage hates the sound of worship. It hates the sound of praise. And it will go out of its way to avoid fellowship. All alone is where it wanted me to be. Instead, I took the time to get closer to the brethren, to realign myself and reconnect. It was a time for me to become strengthened, and unity was the key.

I come up against anger, fury, false passions, and conniptions against Christ. I snuff out hatefulness, resentment, and temper tantrums; ungodly alliances connected to the evil one; relationships and acquaintances designed to pull me to the other side.

I'm letting go, completely, of all of my old offenses: seeds of indignation, contemptuousness, previous bouts of sarcasm, teasing, and especially evil taunts. I command all sneers and glares, along with other tactics used by the enemy to invite me in, to be consumed by His fire. No longer will the enemy use me to spread hate, deceit, and lies.

Instead, I will take refuge in my Father. I'll learn His Word, repeat it, and speak of His glory. It is His voice that I will listen to, and His face that I will continuously seek. I will ask for deliverance, chase after His holiness, and pray for the fruit of the Spirit to be released. Never again will I willingly walk into such a dark place. Holding the hand of the Holy One and being guided by Him, I will not be considered a lost sheep. Forever will I adhere to His calling and follow His voice. In Jesus's name, I pray.

Chapter 6

PRAYER FOR PROTECTION

Put on God's whole armor [the armor of a heavy-armed
soldier which God supplies], that you may be able suc-
cessfully to stand up against [all] the strategies and the
deceits of the devil. For we are not wrestling with flesh
and blood [contending only with physical opponents],
but against the despotisms, against the powers, against
[the master spirits who are] the world rulers of this
present darkness, against the spirit forces of wickedness
in the heavenly (supernatural) sphere.
—EPHESIANS 6:11–12, AMP

FATHER, I PLEAD the blood over my life as I pray for Your protec-
tion. As You lead me, guide me, teach me, and train me, I ask that
You save me from every ambush of the enemy, in the name of Jesus.
Allow my steps to be hidden in the spirit and my presence to go unno-
ticed as I maneuver in what You have called me forth to do. Repel from
me, O God, every plot, plan, and scheme that the enemy has devised spe-
cifically against my life, in the mighty name of Jesus.

Cancel all forms of sickness, bodily aches and pains, and financial
curses. Smite every other form of sickness that is designed to remit my
faith.

Delete accidents, ungodly afflictions and infirmities; oppression,
depression, attacks of lust and perversion, assaults upon and through my
friends, my family, my pets, and my possessions. Erase the creation of
a criminal history, the failure of godly relationships, setbacks, untimely
delays, doubt, and fear.

Cancel the onslaught of pride, boastfulness, and rebellion. Remove
offense, defenselessness, and fear. Protect me, my God, from the backlash,

11

retaliation, and revenge of the enemy. In Jesus's name, shield me from envy, jealousy, and strife.

Answer by fire on my behalf, O God, and come up against those evil things that I cannot see. Let everything that the evil one has arranged in his wayward ways to entrap me, to ensnarl me, and to pull me off course, be consumed by Your fire, in Jesus's name.

Bless me, O God, with a Nehemiah anointing. Teach me to remain focused as You burn up the works of darkness around me. Break in half the darts, the arrows, and the spears that the enemy throws. Cause his weaponry to be dull and unfit to penetrate, useless in every way. Force him, my God, to become the biggest skeptic of his own deeds.

Remind him that he is weak and powerless against me because I belong to You. Let it be known that my defense and refuge is in You, understanding that I wrestle not against flesh and blood, but against principalities and rulers in high places.

My Father, command the enemy to stagger back to his place of business, bruised and empty-handed, to the one that sent him to rival against me. Cause him to be made to return to his sender in a state of confusion—deaf, dumb, unintelligible, blind, and incapacitated; utterly and completely out of control.

Let the one that he follows beat upon his head repeatedly for returning void of any gain. Embarrassed and in shame, call forth a public humiliation, degradation for all of his cohorts to see.

Let the power of Your anger be released upon the powers of darkness warring against me. Punish those who attempt to oppress me. Bring the princes to nothing. I thank You that the devil is defeated and the ruler of evil has been conquered. In Jesus's name, I pray. Amen.

PART II
NOT EASILY BROKEN

Chapter 7

PRAYER AGAINST UNGODLY CONNECTIONS

And show your own self in all respects to be a pattern
and a model of good deeds and works, teaching what
is unadulterated, showing gravity [having the strictest
regard for truth and purity of motive], with dignity
and seriousness. And let your instruction be sound and
fit and wise and wholesome, vigorous and irrefutable
and above censure, so that the opponent may be put
to shame, finding nothing discrediting or evil to say
about us....It has trained us to reject and renounce
all ungodliness (irreligion) and worldly (passionate)
desires, to live discreet (temperate, self-controlled),
upright, devout (spiritually whole) lives in this present
world....Tell [them all] these things. Urge (advise, en-
courage, warn) and rebuke with full authority. Let no
one despise or disregard or think little of you [conduct
yourself and your teaching so as to command respect].
—TITUS 2:7–8, 12, 15, AMP

SEPARATE ME, FATHER, from ungodly connections, unrighteous
relationships, and wickedness that lies dormant in the hearts of
men. Break apart previous promises and alliances that would otherwise lead to mass destruction in my life. Command these principalities,
on my behalf, to become detached, disconnected, and unassociated with
me. Cause them, my Father, to be completely out of their jurisdiction
with no rights to me, my family, or my friends.

In the name of Jesus, let it be known that I want nothing to do with
ungodly connections. Let it be seen that I have stayed far, far away from

them. Today, I live willingly and wholeheartedly under Your ordinances. For it is unto Your laws and Your statutes that I wish to be true. Abide in me, as I abide in You, Father. Allow what was once in the past to be done away with, severed, and completely disconnected from my life. Show me how to achieve the pattern and a model of good deeds and works, leading a lifestyle that exemplifies what is Your unadulterated truth. From You, I want to learn the strictest regard for purity of motive with dignity that is serious in nature.

Let Your instruction be sound and fit. Wise and whole is how I want to be made. Cause the enemy to experience shame for reporting that he could find nothing in me that is discreditable, deliberately vile, evil, or vain. And when he reports back to his master that there were no findings, let him be dealt with severely.

I reject ungodliness and renounce worldly desires. I pray for the guidance to lead a discreet life, upright and devoted [to You]. Allow my daily actions, as I come and go, to bring light to Your name. In Jesus's name, I pray.

Chapter 8

PRAYER AGAINST SABOTAGE

Contend, O Lord, with those who contend with me;
fight against those who fight against me! Take hold of
shield and buckler, and stand up for my help! Draw out
also the spear and javelin and close up the way of those
who pursue and persecute me. Say to me, I am your
deliverance! Let them be put to shame and dishonor
who seek and require my life; let them be turned back
and confounded who plan my hurt! Let them be as
chaff before the wind, with the Angel of the Lord driv-
ing them on! Let their way be through dark and slip-
pery places, with the Angel of the Lord pursuing and
afflicting them. For without cause they hid for me their
net; a pit of destruction without cause they dug for my
life. Let destruction befall [my foe] unawares; let the
net he hid for me catch him; let him fall into that very
destruction.
—PSALM 35:1–8, AMP

FATHER, CANCEL THE assignments used to drive people to abort
progress and success of divinely ordained projects, to put a stop
to and block purposeful relationships within the kingdom. Halt
all activity that leads to the stirring up of jealousy, resentment, and suspicion. Please, Father, put a choke hold on any and everything that is
released through words, thoughts, and actions with the intent of being
vindictive, especially as it relates to the person who detects its presence.

I ask that You attach a boomerang to the butt of sabotage as I command only its sender to be recognized as both victim and perpetrator.

17

When judgment is passed on others through a spirit of sabotage, let it be the same judgment that exposes them in exchange.

Cut all puppet strings, in the mighty name of Jesus, that this spirit uses to skillfully manipulate and control its prey. Let the hands of the enemy be bare, unprotected, and easily identified in the spirit. Cover the one that it operates through with Your blood; cleanse him, wash him, turn him around, and use him instead for Your good. I realize, Father, that this spirit can operate through those who sincerely love me, just as it did in Matthew 16:21–23, where Peter attempted to sabotage the mission of Jesus.

Therefore, Lord, I ask You for victory over this spirit. Lift the veil from my spiritual eyes and allow the scales of deception to fall. Let me see clearly in the spirit only that which You would have me to see. Let everything that is false, intentionally untrue, and kept hidden as a detrimental secret crumble in its own evilness. Cause it, O God, to evaporate, dissipate, completely break down, and disappear. Let only Your truth prevail…Your wisdom and authority.

Protect me, my pets, and my possessions from its lies, fabrications, falsehoods, and untruths. Protect my family. Protect my friends. Let my name be untouchable in the spirit, as it abides in Yours; let it not be easily tainted, damaged, or broken. Make me strong enough to endure (to the end) everything that this spirit brings. And through it all, I will continue to abide in You.

Right now, I drive away this ugly spirit and chase it far from me. Let it go in haste with anyone remotely associated with it. Give me, O God, the ability to spot it miles away. Grant me, O God, the opportunity to reveal openly the secrets of its heart. Force it to be cast down and done away with, only to be picked up again and rebuilt for Your good—that is, only if You see fit.

Father, these things that come to make me stronger, I accept. These things that come to make me wise, I accept, but only from You! Help me to understand Your ways as You teach me and train me. Help me to use Your wisdom as I carry out the tasks assigned. Uncover and help me to discover the strength that You have placed in my hands to do Your good works according to Your will.

Lord, I ask that my spiritual eyes and ears be opened as I take direction and correction from You. Teach me to operate in Your timing and according to Your will as You pull out the enemy's ulterior motives against my life by the root and slay every spirit of scorn and mockery that comes up against me.

Sway me, O God, to react only in Your way as You place a Holy Ghost force field against all activities of derailment, indignation, and arrows shot at me laced with defeat. Cancel the implementation of confusion, slander, and strife. Input Your wisdom where rivalry wants to reign. Enforce Your power and authority over psychological games. Defeat every diabolical trap and scheme that the enemy has planned to set against me.

I only ask that Your presence be near as I commit on a new level to do Your will. Restore me. Revitalize me and awaken me daily in Your goodness and Your grace as I travel to and fro. Let this suffering seem to last but only for one night as I cling to Your Word for encouragement.

Father, I ask that You allow the spirit of a true intercessor to rest upon me as I intercede on behalf of others. Let only Your truth be told and the box of hidden secrets be opened. Let my love for You grow in new dimensions as I lean on You and depend upon You, forevermore. In Jesus's name, I pray.

Chapter 9

PRAYER AGAINST THE SPIRIT OF SATIRE

Boasters can have no standing in Your sight; You
abhor all evildoers. You will destroy those who speak
lies; the Lord abhors [and rejects] the bloodthirsty and
deceitful man.
—Psalm 5:5–6, amp

RIGHT NOW, IN the name of Jesus, I break the back of the spirit of
satire and body slam all of its entanglements of unholy alliances,
treacheries, and gossip to the floor. I overthrow this spirit to a dis-
tance far away from me and put an end to its afflictions in my life. Cause
it, O God, to burn up and disintegrate with Your fire. Let this spirit not
be utilized to cause torment to another.

Ignorantly, I've looked at it for too long. Unknowingly, I've enter-
tained it. For this, my God, I repent. Lead me, Father, in Your wisdom,
and cover me with Your grace. Allow me to draw strength from You
through those that You've allowed to surround me.

I cast down the covenant made with the spirit of satire and break
every agreement that I've ever made with it. I draw a line in the spirit that
it dare not cross over to completely separate myself from its strife.

Prideful you are, shameless and without conviction in all of your ways.
It is in your revengefulness that you will pay. I have no tears for you,
Satire, as you catch the wrath of God. And I will fail to watch in delight
as He penalizes you for your wrongdoings. Know that my heart is not
joyful as you learn from your mistakes. Go from me, do no harm to
anyone else, and abort yourself of such idiosyncrasies.

I repent to the Lord for having anything to do with the spirit of satire
knowingly, or unknowingly; willingly, or unwillingly. For that, I beg for

my Father's forgiveness. Now that I know, now that I understand better, I realize that I am held accountable. Therefore, I pray:

Father, teach me to man my gates better. Imbed within me Your wisdom, Your power, and Your continued grace. Allow me to take on Your authority as I beseech the enemy to go the other way.

First, I'll make supplications to You. Then, I shall gird up to strike: to smite the evil one...to knock his head off! And I will slay him again and again until he comes for me no more.

As I fight, Father, I ask that You would protect the innocent, the unlearned, and those that are perhaps too eager to make a new friend. Protect those that are terribly perceived as unsuspecting because they are living a life of righteousness according to Your will. Protect those, O Lord, who have little or no discernment, those empty of Your boldness, and the destitute of Your Word, as You reveal without forsaking them what is honorable and what is true.

Meanwhile, I too shall stand in fear of Your judgment with remembrance of Your Word according to Romans 2:2 ("But we are sure that the judgment of God is according to truth against them which commit such things"[KJV]).

Again, I will make supplication, but this time more earnest for You. I will praise You. I will worship You. I'll continue to adore You. Forever I will reverence You, Father. In Jesus's name, I pray.

Chapter 10

PRAYER AGAINST DISTRACTIONS

Then I observed all the work and ambition motivated
by envy. What a waste! Smoke. And spitting into the
wind. The fool sits back and takes it easy, His sloth is
slow suicide.
—ECCLESIASTES 4:4–5, THE MESSAGE

ATHER, I BESEECH You to close every trap door of the enemy, in
the name of Jesus. Everything that comes to beset me, rearrange
things in my life, discourage, and bring discontentment, let it be
removed.

Cancel every spirit of foul play in my life, spiritual abortion, spirit
of the backstabber, spirit of the bastard, and spirits of witchcraft. Cause
them to be gone once and for all.

Shut the mouth, O God, of every naysayer, the ones who breed con-
tention and strife. Close the gate of every entry point in my life where
the enemy attempts to creep in. Every spirit unlike the Holy Spirit that is
sent on assignment against me, let it be ruined. Help me to rise against
the one that comes to cause things not to be done right as You order my
steps opposite of the one that goes against You. Allow not the spirit of
distraction to take steps with me, for we fail miserably to walk together
in unison or agreement as one.

No more excuses will I make of myself for not being ready, prepared, and in position when You call. I have put away every unwarranted
apology. And no more defenses will I carry for being unable to do Your
will. Equip me and train me, Father, for I am Yours to keep.

Snatch the culprit by the neck; the one that wants to steal my praise,
my honor, and my worship for You. Crack the back of the one who comes

to take away my deliverance as You allow it to become common knowledge to every enemy that I love You more.

Protect me, O God, from every lustful spirit that wants to find its way into my heart; every greedy spirit, every hoarding spirit, and every perverse spirit that is displeasing to You. I will continue to tithe. I will continue to give You my best. I will continue to live my life according to Your statues, because my salvation has never been, nor ever will be, up for trade.

Daily I will submit; ask that I be made to die to the flesh; give of my time, my money, my talents, and every effort afforded to me, in turn, to Your kingdom. And may I be reminded of Your goodness, Your grace, and the mercies that You bring, knowing that this time I won't get weary.

As each day goes by, I pray that we grow closer, stronger, and more in love than ever. In my daily walk with Jesus, cause me to be suitable to resist temptations designed to trick me into breaking my vows unto You. Hide me in Your pavilion as the persecution persists. And allow me to rest in You as the devourer reaches for my neck.

Thank You, God, for placing Your protective shield around me that makes me untouchable to my enemies. Thank You for delivering me from distractions that keep me from focusing on You. Thank You, Father. I bless Your holy name. In Jesus's name, I pray. Amen.

Chapter 11

NO NEED FOR ANOTHER

Say to skillful and godly Wisdom, You are my sister, and regard understanding or insight as your intimate friend—That they may keep you from the loose woman, from the adventuress who flatters with and makes smooth her words. For at the window of my house I looked out through my lattice. And among the simple (empty-headed and emptyhearted) ones, I perceived among the youths a young man void of good sense, Sauntering through the street near the [loose woman's] corner; and he went the way to her house. In the twilight, in the evening; night black and dense was falling [over the young man's life]. And behold, there met him a woman, dressed as a harlot and sly and cunning of heart. She is turbulent and willful; her feet stay not in her house. Now in the streets, now in the marketplaces, she sets her ambush at every corner. So she caught him and kissed him and with impudent face she said to him, Sacrifices of peace offerings were due from me; this day I paid my vows. So I came forth to meet you [that you might share with me the feast from my offering]; diligently I sought your face, and I have found you. I have spread my couch with rugs and cushions of tapestry, with striped sheets of fine linen of Egypt. I have perfumed my bed with myrrh, aloes, and cinnamon. Come, let us take our fill of love until morning; let us console and delight ourselves with love. For the man is not at home; he is gone on a long journey; He has taken a bag of money with him and will come home at the day appointed [at the full moon]. With much justifying and enticing argument she persuades him, with the allurements of her lips she leads him [to overcome his conscience and his fears] and forces him along. Suddenly he [yields and] follows her reluctantly like

an ox moving to the slaughter, like one in fetters going
to the correction [to be given] to a fool or like a dog
enticed by food to the muzzle. Till a dart [of passion]
pierces and inflames his vitals; then like a bird flutter-
ing straight into the net [he hastens], not knowing that
it will cost him his life. Listen to me now therefore, O
you sons, and be attentive to the words of my mouth.
Let not your heart incline toward her ways, do not stray
into her paths. For she has cast down many wounded;
indeed, all her slain are a mighty host. Her house is
the way to Sheol (Hades, the place of the dead), going
down to the chamber of death.
—PROVERBS 7:4–27, AMP

I USED TO THINK that I had a need for another; another drink, another
smoke, another empty relationship leading to disaster; another heart-
ache, another heartbreak, another delusion, and another "unhappy
ever after."

Another body blow to my inner man, another uppercut to his chin;
another backslide, another encounter; ultimately, a remarriage to my
deepest sin. Another kept calling me, leaving messages of fornication. I
was blinded by spirits of deafness and dumbness, too eager to satisfy my
flesh. I was always in the wrong place, at the wrong time, with the wrong
people, for all of the wrong reasons. Yet, I wondered: "How did Another
get my number? How is it that he calls me by name?"

Another would sit on my shoulders and go to work with me every day.
He'd play games and talk to me, but never listened to what I had to say.

"I want to be free of you!" I told him. But Another didn't care.

"Here. Take these pills, sleep your way through sadness, and finally
give up, as I drown you in fear."

Another was evil, very enticing, sometimes appealing, and beyond per-
suasive to say the least. Another was full of pain and suffering. Another
was a beast. I got caught up in Another, entangled in his evil deeds and
his ways. We slept together in uncleanliness and impurities. We bathed

together in social isolation, emotional victimization, and severe self-consciousness. Another embarrassed me and controlled me. He fed me a diet of guilt, shame, and distress every day.

So, yeah, I had another drink, another smoke, another empty relationship leading to disaster. Again, I was met with heartaches, heartbreaks, letdowns, and a slew of disappointments, followed by a host of diabolical disasters.

The works of the flesh were all over me and I did not know what to do. "How did these things get into me?" I asked. "Whom can I turn to?"

> For [The Spirit which] you have now received [is] not a spirit of slavery to put you once more in bondage to fear, but you have received the Spirit of adoption [the Spirit producing sonship] in [the bliss of] which we cry, Abba (Father)! Father!
> —Romans 8:15, amp

"Abba Father, Abba Father!" I cried, and immediately He took me in. It is because of Abba Father, my Daddy God, that I am no longer a slave to my sins. For this I thank You, Abba. In Jesus's name, I pray. Amen.

PART III
BECOMING FORTIFIED

Chapter 12

PRAYER OF DEPENDENCE

Fear not [there is nothing to fear], for I am with you;
do not look around you in terror and be dismayed, for
I am your God. I will strengthen and harden you to dif-
ficulties, yes, I will help you; yes, I will hold you up and
retain you with My [victorious] right hand of rightness
and justice.
—Isaiah 41:10, amp

I BLESS YOUR HOLY name, Father, no matter what the situation; no
matter what the circumstances; no matter what the costs. With You
is where I want to be. I'll continue to chase after You, full force, with
a strong desire to be with You, in You, and around You, in Jesus's name.

I'll beseech You, always wanting and needing You; forever thirsty for
Your Word, and even more hungry for Your presence; committed to the
task; obligated to the call, tied to and trusting in You for it. I am duty-
bound to You, Father, as abiding in You has made me virtually immune
to the temptations offered to me by darkness.

Lost and unfortunate is what I am without You; aware of the torment
that awaits me if I should ever choose to turn my face from Thee. Set me
apart. Separate me again unto You. Becoming completely detached and
unassociated from that which does not include You is fine by me.

Invite me in, Father. Allow me to lean and depend on You as You
handle my current situation. For I recognize that I am far too small to
rectify any of it in and of myself. I need You!

I will take refuge in Your Word as I rely upon You for the appropriate
response. What do I do? How do I handle this matter in the right way?
These are the questions that must be answered by You. And as I wait for
Your answer, I ask that You release my mind from the traps set by the

enemy to prompt worry. Cause my memory of previous disappointments to fade. Convert my scent [in the spirit] to be the nonequivalent of a spirit that adheres to sorrow as You put the enemy to shame.

Humbly, I ask for a reminder of what *not* to say as You work things out on my behalf. Lying still and quiet is the posture that I shall keep as I wait. These are the experiences that help my love for You to become tightly interlaced with a level of faith and trust that squeezes out doubt, baffles panic, and crucifies spirits of dismay. My destiny has always been and shall forever remain in Your hands, Lord.

Whatever You tell me to do, I will do it. Wherever You send me, I will go without a murmur or a complaint. My responses to every situation are based on Your input, Your opinion, and Your reply, as my allegiance to You grows deeper. Father, I thank You now for the strength that You have given me to handle the outcome. In Jesus's name, I pray. Amen.

Chapter 13

PRAYER AGAINST FEAR

O Lord, rebuke me not in Your anger nor discipline
and chasten me in Your hot displeasure. Have mercy on
me and be gracious to me, O Lord, for I am weak (faint
and withered away); O Lord, heal me, for my bones are
troubled. My [inner] self [as well as my body] is also
exceedingly disturbed and troubled. But You, O Lord,
how long [until You return and speak peace to me]?
Return [to my relief], O Lord, deliver my life; save me
for the sake of Your steadfast love and mercy. For in
death there is no remembrance of You; in Sheol (the
place of the dead) who will give You thanks? I am weary
with my groaning; all night I soak my pillow with tears,
I drench my couch with my weeping. My eye grows
dim because of grief; it grows old because of all my enemies. Depart from them, all you workers of iniquity, for
the Lord has heard the voice of my weeping. The Lord
has heard my supplication; the Lord receives my prayer.
Let all my enemies be ashamed and sore troubled; let
them turn back and be put to shame suddenly.
—PSALM 6:1–10, AMP

I COME UP AGAINST all forms of fear that have been sent against my
life, in the mighty name of Jesus. I pull down every stronghold, every
setback, every setup, and every repeat of exaggeration forwarded to
me by the enemy.

I tear down the fort that the enemy has raised against me; disperse his
cohorts and force them each to abort their assignment against my name.
Bring shame upon them, Father, for participating in such tactics.

31

Release Your warring angels to fight on my behalf as I war against fear. All forms of dread, doubt, and dismay, I command you to go. Every spirit of timidity and frailty will be a part of me no more. To the end I war against you with the Lord of hosts on my side. I decree and declare that the sword of the Lord shall prevail.

Insecurities, be gone. Nightmares, be gone. Cries of terror, shame, and self-condemnation, be gone, right now, in the name of Jesus. Fear of what people think, be gone. Fear of what people say, be gone. Fear of making the wrong decision, fear of being alone, and fear of suffering, go, right now, in Jesus's name.

I cast down every spirit that comes to manipulate and torment me, every spirit that advocates self-isolation and self-containment. I cast down every spirit of extreme shyness, oversensitivity, doubt, mistrust, and fear, in the name of Jesus. I cast you down and I plead the blood over my thoughts.

And I thank You, Father, that You have not given me the spirit of fear, but of power, love, and a sound mind. I thank You that the torment has gone from me and peace is my portion. In Jesus's name, I pray. Amen.

Chapter 14

PRAYER FOR MY SALVATION

For it is by free grace (God's unmerited favor) that you
are saved (delivered from judgment and made partakers
of Christ's salvation) through [your] faith. And this [sal-
vation] is not of yourselves [of your own doing, it came
not through your own striving], but it is the gift of
God; Not because of works [not the fulfillment of the
Law's demands], lest any man should boast. [It is not
the result of what anyone can possibly do, so no one
can pride himself in it or take glory to himself.] For we
are God's [own] handiwork (His workmanship), recre-
ated in Christ Jesus, [born anew] that we may do those
good works which God predestined (planned before-
hand) for us [taking paths which He prepared ahead of
time], that we should walk in them [living the good life
which He prearranged and made ready for us to live.]
—EPHESIANS 2:8–10, AMP

L ORD, I THANK You for Your salvation, which delivers me from all
evil. I thank You for Your gifts of grace that save me by faith, the
truth and new life [for me] that is in You. I thank You, heavenly
Father, Prince of Peace, for the day that You died for my sins, was buried,
and rose again. I thank You for Your love, Your mercy, Your tender loving-
kindness. I thank You for forgiving my sins, and for teaching me to know
that You will never leave nor forsake me. For these things, I thank You.

It is through prayer and daily supplication that I invite You in as
my personal Lord and Savior, Ruler over my life from beginning until
the end. Every day that You allow me to awaken is an opportunity to
share with You how just You are, how righteous, good, and true. There

is nothing in and of myself that could ever match the gift that You have given me. It is Your salvation that promises me life everlasting. Safe. Protected. Provided and cared for. Loved. Redeemed and spiritually nurtured. Delivered from evil and living in truth. Looked upon as beloved and precious in Your sight. No reason shall I ever find to leave You. I am restored, rejuvenated, and completely comforted in every area of my life, taking refuge in You and able to relax with You during the storms that situations and circumstances sometimes bring. No man on earth could ever be this good [to me].

I admit that I have sinned; therefore, I am a sinner. For the things that I have done and now leave behind, it is to You that I repent. I believe, with the faith that You have provided, that Jesus Christ died for me, was buried, and rose from the dead. I invite You into my heart and accept You as my personal Lord and Savior.

Allow me to take these first steps with You, as You lead me into Your kingdom. Guard me as I read Your Word every day in an effort to get to know You better. Protect me from that which comes to block the flow of our worship, our fellowship, the essence of what brings us together as one. Cause us, Father, to unite and bond strongly in and of one another.

Make me strong to carry out Your will, to live according to Your statutes, and to give You pure praise. Let the best in me be brought out through Your salvation. I acknowledge You as the Consuming Fire in my life, the Creator of heaven and earth, the One who forgives my sins and saves me. You are the God of all comfort, the God of grace, and the One that I cry out to when I am feeling somber. To You, my personal Savior, I give praise. In Jesus's name, I pray. Amen.

Chapter 15

PRAYER FOR SEPARATION, CONSECRATION, AND DELIVERANCE

All the days of his separation and abstinence he is holy
to the Lord.
—NUMBERS 6:8, AMP

THANK YOU FOR the separation, consecration, and deliverance that brings me closer to You. Thank You for holding me accountable to a new level of righteousness as I beseech You daily for guidance. Father, I ask that You purify me. Purify my heart, my mind, and my soul. Please purify the thoughts that I think in an effort to give You more pure worship. Help me to uncover hidden truths about myself as I seek Your face. In our private time together, reveal to me what is close to Your heart.

I thank You for the separation. Let it be recognized by those who love me as a time that I am not lonely. Do not let it be mistaken as self-imposed isolation; by far, that is not the truth.

It is a time for my heart to be filled with the joy and happiness that comes from knowing You better; the explanations received that provide understanding, the wisdom that is imparted, and the grace that I need from You. It is a time of spiritual nurturing, developing, and maturation. And I thank You for every time that we commune together—connect— and You open Your arms wide to allow me in.

I plead the blood over the times that You have designated for complete separation, consecration, and deliverance between You and me. I know, recognize, and thoroughly understand that in no way could I say or do anything to allure such a benefit on my own. It is because of You that I have received an invitation to be treasured. And I do value You.

Father, please act as my rear guard as I come to You again and again

35

for further development. Protect me from the effects of envy and strife. Warn all spirits of gossip and idle thinking to go away. Shield me, my Father, from anything that comes to block me from getting to You.

In Jesus's name, I bow down before You and give You reverence. For the things that You teach me during these times, I know to be true. Awaken in me, Father, a new side that identifies with Your godliness, Your sanctity, and Your holiness. Intensify me, O God, in every part of You.

My desire is to be used for Your glory. Let my actions be a clear reflection of who You are on the inside of me. Let Your word of wisdom chasten me as I thank You for the chastisement.

I bind myself to You, O God. Let Your thoughts become my thoughts. Let Your ways become my ways. Take me into Your private chambers. Let me enter daily as I wholeheartedly come with a strong desire to be made more like You.

Break me, if You have to. Purge me. Prune me. Take out the old and put in the new. Anoint my eyes to see You better. Intensify my hearing to hear You all the more. Come in and change the way that I walk in life. Alter my speech, my thinking, and my whole way of being. Pivot my lifestyle into a position that is pleasing to You.

And through every transition and every transaction that You allow, pass or fail, know that I will run back to You. For with You is where I want to be. It is in Jesus's name I pray. Amen.

Chapter 16

PRAYER FOR TRANSFORMATION

> And You [He made alive], when you were dead (slain)
> by [your] trespasses and sins. In which at one time you
> walked [habitually]. You were following the course and
> fashion of this world [were under the sway of the ten-
> dency of this present age], following the prince of the
> power of the air. [You were obedient to and under the
> control of the [demon] spirit that still constantly works
> in the sons of disobedience [the careless, the rebellious,
> and the unbelieving, who go against the purposes of
> God]. Among these we as well as you once lived and
> conducted ourselves in the passions of our flesh [our
> behavior governed by our corrupt and sensual nature],
> obeying the impulses of the flesh and the thoughts of
> the mind [our cravings dictated by our senses and our
> dark imaginings]. We were then by nature children of
> [God's] wrath and heirs of [His] indignation, like the
> rest of mankind.
> —EPHESIANS 2:1–3, AMP

LORD, CHANGE MY mind about the things that I say, the words that I speak, the duties that I carry out, and the people that I am around. Change my mind, O God, when it comes to the thoughts that I think, the places that I go, and every deed that is in my life but not in Your will for me.

My Lord and Savior, Protector and Provider, the Deliverer of my soul, please change my way of thinking, my way of doing. Change me. Shape me. Make me to be a godly configuration. Transform me into exactly who You are calling me forth to be. Change my identity as I agree to open up to new experiences, new developments, and new people. Teach me how to not close the door to what would otherwise have blossomed into wonderful and caring relationships. Cause me, O God, to make a friend because of You.

Spirits of timidity and shyness are now far from me. The very residue of what once caused me to be fainthearted is now dead and gone. No longer am I fearful. I have You to bless for that.

Open my eyes, O God, to the good things that I have yet to imagine, to become excited in life about, and to fully and deliberately experience. Bless me with the fullness of Your transformation in my life: my heart, my mind, my way of being, seeing, thinking, knowing, and doing.

No more excuses will I make to You to run the other way when another soul comes close to me. I will not flee from that which is new and different, holding the possibility of something unexpectedly pleasant and good. Prepare me to step into new settings and a new way of doing things in You. Let both Your power and authority be the leading force that guides me.

Lead my mouth to speak words of Your goodness, Your mercy, and not of tragedies that would disgrace You. Allow the appearance of my inner beauty to be appealing—appealing enough to draw others to become interested in *You*. Holy Spirit, I pray that as others encounter me, You will speak sweet words to them that my lips could never say.

Bind my mind to Your mind; my thoughts to Your thoughts; my ways to Your will for my life. Let my character and Your attributes become one. I'll confide in You and continue to commune with You. Forever I will honor You. In Jesus's name, I pray. Amen.

Chapter 17

IT'S OK TO LOVE

Above all things have intense and unfailing love for one
another, for love covers a multitude of sins [forgives
and disregards the offenses of others.]
—1 PETER 4:8, AMP

THERE WAS A time, once, when I felt free to love—to give love, to
receive love, to be in love and not without it. Then, suddenly, life
changed. As I got older, a series of events came along and swal-
lowed my love whole, where it was kept captive for decades.

My heart was frozen solid in one place because it had become petrified
by what others had done. Rigid and inactive, [my heart] sat locked away
for years. Crushed by devastating feats with death of loved ones, over-
whelmed by the guilt and the shame, I chose, instead, to sit in darkness,
hoping that no one would recognize me.

During the daylight, I walked in fear; the sufferer of the terror by
night. In silence I held it all in, hoping to endure. But never did that
work. How could it?

So now I pray:

Thank You, Lord. My heart is no longer filled with
stones of malice. Hardness of the heart is no longer
my portion. So glad am I for the day that You found me—
the day that I let You in. You have delivered me. I am free
to love; to give love, to receive love; to be in love, and
never without it. Again, You have saved me. I am thankful
to You always. Thanks to You, I have been released from
insecurities, no longer bound by apathy. My heart is free
to care, to share, and even to imagine. Joy is in me because
of You.

Cause my heart to become filled with integrity and innocence daily; keep [my heart] guarded and safe. In the name of Jesus, sentence to death the one that comes to taint or corrupt it. Punish them severely. Embed forgiveness in my heart, repentance, patience, and humility. Restore it. Heal it. Deliver it. Saturate it until it is completely full of faith and hope in You. Reveal to me, Father, the things that will make [my heart] clean and true to You.

I trust You. I believe You and I will love You forever more. In Jesus's name, I pray. Amen.

Chapter 18

PRAYER OF OBEDIENCE

There you will serve gods, the work of men's hands,
wood and stone, which neither see nor hear nor eat nor
smell. But if from there you will seek (inquire for and
require as necessity) the Lord your God, you will find
Him if you [truly] seek Him with all your heart [and
mind] and soul and life.
—DEUTERONOMY 4:28–29, AMP

To You, MY Father, I relinquish all rights to my life. Please break
down the strongholds, the walls, the barriers, and every blockade
that the enemy has set to keep me from getting to You. My desire
is for You to have full and complete control over every area and every
aspect of my life.

Willfully, I agree to participate in experiences that promise to manifest Your goodness and Your glory. With this, I agree to be fully exposed
to the soreness that sometimes comes from Your wrath. For Your chastisement is not only necessary, it is wanted and needed.

Impart to me Your will; although, many times the details of its ingre-
dients will surpass my minute means of understanding. Make my life to
pattern Your perfection; cause my hands to be judged *not guilty* because
they have been washed clean in the Spirit. Allow my whole life and all
that I encounter to be the resting place that reaps rewards of Your influ-
ence over me; that which entails an unshakable and deliberate ordination
of obedience. Let the covenant of my obedience be connected to You
unto death, in Jesus's name.

I have asked You for success and prosperity in the spirit, as well as
in the natural. I have prayed to You for peace, joy, rest, and happiness,
victory over my enemies, good health, and long life. Let not Your com-

PETITIONS TO MY FATHER

mandments be made grievous nor heavy upon my heart, but instead, I ask that You smile upon me. Take my hand and guide me through a lifestyle of obedience that pleases You; one that is not blind in nature, but fortified by Your strength because it is true. Mate my lineage to be fit to breed in the obedience of the righteous.

Wash away all that is within me that is old, stagnant, and must be replaced. Uproot wickedness to allow a new thing [in You] to be planted, watered, and nurtured with loving care so that it may grow. Cause it, my Father, to grow in me, for me, and all around me. And let that growth be wondrously contagious.

In addition, intensify my hearing to a point that it can easily drown out doubt and amplify Your voice. Loud and clear is how I must be made to hear You. Precise! Correct! On point! Accurate!

Father, I thank You for every entry point provided that allows me to enter into You—every exchange, every encounter, every impartation. I ask that You sharpen my discernment and increase my faith so that I may stand strong in what I have been called to do. Please bless me with Your wisdom, Your knowledge, and another level of understanding. Allow me to once again receive Your grace. I will follow You forever, compliant and submissive to the laws that You have set before me. In Jesus's name, I pray. Amen.

Chapter 19

I WANT

Do not fret or have any anxiety about anything, but in
every circumstance and in everything, by prayer and
petition (definite requests), with thanksgiving, continue
to make your wants known to God.
—Philippians 4:6, amp

O fear the Lord, you His saints [revere and worship
Him]! For there is no want to those who truly revere
and worship Him with godly fear.
—Psalm 34:9, amp

I want Your goodness.
I want Your grace.
I want Your everlasting mercy.
I want Your will to be done in my life, in the name of Jesus.
I want a relationship with You, Father; one that is true and everlasting.
I want to suffer through You and reign with You.
I want to talk to You, knowing that You listen.
I want to hear every word that You speak to me, knowing that it is true.
I want to follow You.
I want Your comfort.
I want Your input and Your opinion.
I want You to hold my hand and guide me through life, as I trust You
like I could no man on earth.

With each test and trial that I have to encounter, I want Your voice to
be the one that whispers the answers.

I want to be in You, for You, with You, and of You. I want more of
You. In Jesus's name, I pray.

43

Chapter 20

CRIES OF A WARRIOR

For the weapons of our warfare are not physical [weapons of flesh and blood], but they are mighty before God for the overthrow and destruction of strongholds.
—2 CORINTHIANS 10:4, AMP

IN THE MIGHTY name of Jesus, I uproot every evil seed that the enemy intends to plant in my life. I command each seed to be cast down and deemed absolutely no good, in the name of Jesus. I demand that every witchcraft prayer spoken against my life go unanswered, and for all spirits of the occult, especially involving soothsaying, to be made incomplete.

Right now, I poke out the eye of the evil one and speak spiritual deafness and dumbness over the one that listens to my prayers with ill intent. Let the sound of my prayers painfully pierce the eardrums of my adversaries.

God of war, I ask that You allow complete chaos and confusion to run rampant in his camp. Cause them, O God, to turn one against the other—biting, scratching, clawing, and ripping at one another until the last demon standing falls to its death.

Raise up a holy havoc in the resting place of my enemies, O God. Cause him to die where he sleeps. As for that which has been conjured up in darkness against me, I ask that it be bought to light, right now, in the mighty name of Jesus.

Let the secret counsel of the wicked not be shared one with the other [as in regard to evil]. But instead, let its source be depleted, dried up, disintegrated, and dispersed, in the mighty name of Jesus. O God, cause his evil plots and plans to be taken completely apart.

Right now, I command that every lie the wicked one intends to tell about me be left unspoken. In the spirit, I snatch those evil words right out of his mouth. In the name of Jesus, I command all evil intent against me to be stripped to pieces and dismantled beyond recognition; torn down, annihilated, and utterly destroyed. Let the cries of the righteous be heard throughout [the spirit]. God, please make the sound so enormous that it cracks the foundation of the kingdom of darkness.

I decree and declare that, as Your end-time warrior, my life is made victorious. I decree and declare that the captives have been set free. I decree and declare that I am complete in Christ (Col. 2:10). I am risen with Christ (Col. 3:1). I am redeemed from the curse of the law (Gal. 3:13). Unrighteous living is broken, bands of wickedness have become unfixed, and the tormentor is now the tormented. For it is in Christ that I triumph (2 Cor. 2:14).

I cover the borders of my existence with the blood of the Lamb and smear it over every doorpost of my life: my home, my car, my pets, and possessions; my occupation, my current deeds, my future aspirations; my friends and family; the words that I speak, the thoughts that I think, the dreams that I have, and my daily living—let them all be covered by the blood of Jesus.

Teach me, Your warrior, to rise up in Jesus's name, to press toward the mark of the high calling of God in Christ. Train me, Father, to raise my sword high in the spirit with righteous hands, a clean heart, and a sound mind. Impress upon me, O God, how to operate in Your power, Your authority, and Your might.

Mighty God, slay the evil one that lies in wait at my doorstep. Defame his unholy name. Cause him to burn up from the inside out by Your fire. For this enemy is wretched, vile and unclean, and only comes to take away.

Let it be known that the Greater One lives on the inside of me. And no weapon formed against me shall prosper and every tongue that rises against me in judgment I condemn (Isa. 54:17). I am the righteousness of God in Christ (2 Cor. 5:21). I am the head and not the tail (Deut. 28:13). I shall decree a thing and it shall be (Job 22:28).

Therefore, I crush, kill, and destroy every egg that the enemy attempts to lay in my life. I speak a spiritual abortion over the symptoms that are used to manifest his lies. His deceitfulness is destroyed. His wickedness has been drained.

I decree and declare that all traps and schemes set by the enemy will be revealed this season as his antics prove to be antiquated and made well

45

known. Demolished is what they are because they have been corrupted by a righteous force.

In the name of Jesus, I come up against backlash, retaliation, and revenge. And I will rise supernaturally above envy, jealousy, and strife. I take dominion over the strongman and strip him of his armor, allowing me to continue to march forward.

I have been given the authority to tread upon the heads of serpents and scorpions (Luke 10:19). My hand is upon the neck of my enemies (Gen. 49:8). I stand in the evil day having my loins girt about with truth, and I have the breastplate of righteousness. My feet are shod with the gospel of peace. I take the shield of faith, I am covered with the helmet of salvation, and I use the sword of the Spirit which is the Word of God (Eph. 6:14–17). I have the victory! In Jesus's name, I pray.

Chapter 21

THANKFUL

O give thanks to the Lord, call on His name; make
known His doings among the peoples!
—1 Chronicles 16:8

R IGHT NOW, O God, I give thanks for all that You do, have done,
and are doing. It is You, Father, who cleanses me of my sins. Your
name is Majestic because You are holy; wonderful and magnifi-
cent You are. With all that is in me, I praise Thee.

It is Your precious blood that washes me clean. Daily shall I give You
honor. I praise You, Father. I worship You. And I bow down to reverence
You, in the name of Jesus.

Allow me into Your secret place. Let me hide inside You forever and
take refuge. Cause me, O God, to be delivered, and to come forward at
Your appointed times to commune with You. I pray that we fellowship
together intimately as one.

I thank You, Father, for the sacrifice that You have made for me. I
bless Your holy name, Jesus of Nazareth, for shielding me from my own
sins. You've introduced me to Your goodness; bestowed upon me Your
grace.

I'll commune with You daily and give no weight to sin as You carry
me through trials, tribulations, and burdens that would be far too much
for me to handle. I'll live a lifestyle, as best I can, that gives glory to Your
name.

Fill me, Father, until I am overflowing in Your Spirit. Allow me to
dance before You until my body grows tired from giving You praise. How
thankful I am that You saved me. You've delivered me. You are my Lord
and Savior. For these things I am truly thankful, and I give You praise
for who You are. In Jesus's name, I pray. Amen.

ABOUT THE AUTHOR

RHODORA JAMES WAS born and raised in northern New Jersey. She holds a degree in court reporting, a BA in speech communications, and she is a graduate of Word Bible College in Jacksonville, Florida.

CONTACT THE AUTHOR

Rhodora James
P.O. Box 9351
Jacksonville, FL 32208